SUPER SCIENCE FEATS:
MEDICAL BREAKTHROUGHS
GERM THEORY

by Alicia Z. Klepeis

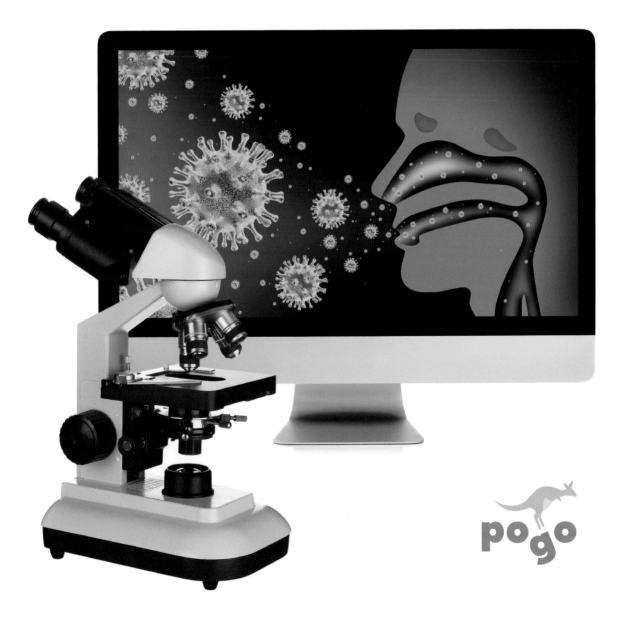

pogo

Ideas for Parents and Teachers

Pogo Books let children practice reading informational text while introducing them to nonfiction features such as headings, labels, sidebars, maps, and diagrams, as well as a table of contents, glossary, and index.

Carefully leveled text with a strong photo match offers early fluent readers the support they need to succeed.

Before Reading

- "Walk" through the book and point out the various nonfiction features. Ask the student what purpose each feature serves.
- Look at the glossary together. Read and discuss the words.

Read the Book

- Have the child read the book independently.
- Invite him or her to list questions that arise from reading.

After Reading

- Discuss the child's questions. Talk about how he or she might find answers to those questions.
- Prompt the child to think more. Ask: Did you know about germs before reading this book? Have you learned new ways to prevent the spread of germs?

Pogo Books are published by Jump!
5357 Penn Avenue South
Minneapolis, MN 55419
www.jumplibrary.com

Library of Congress Cataloging-in-Publication Data

Names: Klepeis, Alicia, 1971- author.
Title: Germ theory / by Alicia Z. Klepeis.
Description: Minneapolis: Jump!, Inc., [2021]
Series: Super science feats: medical breakthroughs
Includes index. | Audience: Ages 7-10
Identifiers: LCCN 2020027743 (print)
LCCN 2020027744 (ebook)
ISBN 9781645277989 (hardcover)
ISBN 9781645277996 (paperback)
ISBN 9781645278009 (ebook)
Subjects: LCSH: Germ theory of disease—Juvenile literature. | Diseases—Causes and theories of causation—Juvenile literature.
Classification: LCC RB153 .K53 2021 (print)
LCC RB153 (ebook) | DDC 571.8/45—dc23
LC record available at https://lccn.loc.gov/2020027743
LC ebook record available at https://lccn.loc.gov/2020027744

Editor: Eliza Leahy
Designer: Michelle Sonnek

Photo Credits: Shutterstock, cover; hamurishi/Shutterstock, 1 (left); Lightspring/Shutterstock, 1 (right); Kittima05/Shutterstock, 3; PaulGregg/iStock, 4; nobeastsofierce/Shutterstock, 5; rolfbodmer/iStock, 6; Heritage Image Partnership Ltd/Alamy, 7; Sueddeutsche Zeitung/Alamy, 8-9; Science History Images/Alamy, 10; The Reading Room/Alamy, 11 (foreground); Albert Fedchenko/Shutterstock, 11 (background); Robbie Ross/iStock, 12-13; Motortion Films/Shutterstock, 14-15; PrasitRodphan/Shutterstock, 16-17; Andy Dean Photography/Shutterstock, 18-19; PeopleImages/iStock, 20-21; exopixel/Shutterstock, 23.

Printed in the United States of America at Corporate Graphics in North Mankato, Minnesota.

TABLE OF CONTENTS

CHAPTER 1

WHAT MAKES US SICK?

Have you ever had a cold? Maybe you've had a stomach bug. What causes these illnesses? For most of history, people did not know.

There were many **theories**. Like what? Some thought evil spirits caused **disease**. Others thought bad smells did! We now know that **germs** cause sickness.

germ

CHAPTER 2

STUDYING GERMS

Scientists were not sure that germs caused illness until the mid-1800s. Microscopes helped. They showed that **microorganisms** existed. This gave scientists an idea. What if these tiny organisms caused diseases? We call this idea **germ theory**.

microscope ·····▶

Louis Pasteur

Proving germ theory was not easy. It took the work of many scientists. Louis Pasteur was one. He found that **bacteria** cause diseases. He called bacteria germs.

Robert Koch took this idea further. How? He proved that a certain bacteria could directly cause a disease. He **identified** the one that caused **tuberculosis**. Pasteur and Koch get much of the credit for germ theory. But many others helped, too.

DID YOU KNOW?

The idea that microorganisms cause disease has been around for a long time. Scientist Marcus Varro lived in ancient Rome. He had this idea more than 2,000 years ago.

Robert
Koch

CHAPTER 3

HOW GERMS SPREAD

Germ theory says that germs cause illness. Germs come from sick people. They spread to others. But how? A doctor named John Snow discovered one way.

John Snow

In 1854, **cholera** spread through London, England. Snow studied it. What did he learn? Many sick people had drunk water from the same pump. Cholera had spread through **polluted** water.

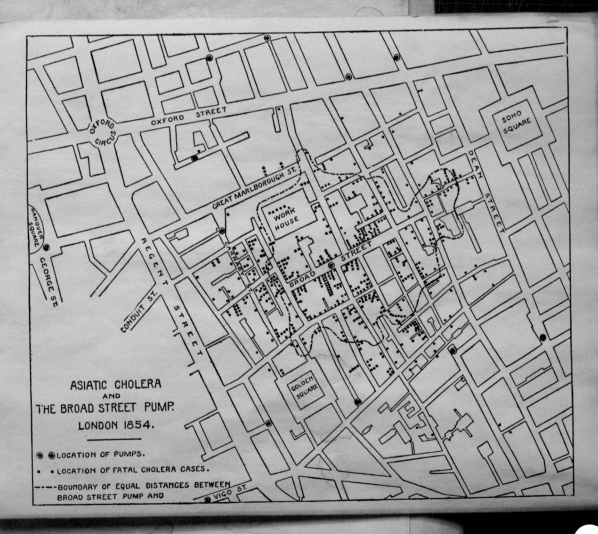

ASIATIC CHOLERA
AND
THE BROAD STREET PUMP.
LONDON 1854.

● ◉ LOCATION OF PUMPS.
• • LOCATION OF FATAL CHOLERA CASES.
- - - BOUNDARY OF EQUAL DISTANCES BETWEEN BROAD STREET PUMP AND

To get sick, germs must enter your body. How? They can come in through your nose, eyes, or mouth. They can enter through cuts in your skin. They can also spread in the air.

TAKE A LOOK!

How do germs spread in the air? Take a look!

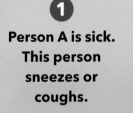

①
Person A is sick. This person sneezes or coughs.

②
Germs enter the air.

③
Person B breathes in the air. Germs enter person B's body.

④
The germs multiply. Person B gets sick.

Germs can live on surfaces for days. A person who is sick might touch a doorknob. You touch the knob after that person. If you then rub your eyes, the germs can enter your body. You might get sick.

DID YOU KNOW?

Germs are all around us. A single germ can multiply into more than eight million germs in just one day. Wow!

You can help keep germs to yourself. How? Washing your hands is the best way. Our hands spread almost 80 percent of germs that cause sickness. **Hand sanitizer** is another option when soap and water are not available.

DID YOU KNOW?

It is important to dry your hands well. Why? Damp hands spread 1,000 times more germs!

How else can you stop the spread of sicknesses like the common cold and COVID-19? Cough or sneeze into your elbow. Use **PPE**. Wear gloves. Keep your distance from others. How much distance? Doctors say at least six feet (1.8 meters).

Many doctors suggest wearing a face mask or shield. If everyone wears one, the spread of sickness slows.

Germ theory helped us understand what causes disease. It also helped us understand how germs spread. It was a medical **breakthrough**. Germ theory made it easier to stay healthy. You have Pasteur, Koch, and many other scientists to thank!

ACTIVITIES & TOOLS

GLITTER AND GERMS

Find out how effective soap is at getting rid of germs in this activity. The pepper or glitter are used to represent germs.

What You Need:

- water
- a baking dish
- a teaspoon
- black pepper or glitter
- hand soap or dishwashing liquid

1. Pour water into the baking dish until it is about half full.

2. Sprinkle a teaspoon or two of pepper or glitter onto the surface of the water.

3. Dip your unwashed finger into the center of the water. What happens to the pepper or glitter?

4. Dry your finger completely. Then coat your finger in a layer of soap or dishwashing liquid.

5. Dip your soapy finger into the water. What happens to the pepper or glitter this time?

bacteria: Single-celled microorganisms that exist everywhere and that can either be useful or harmful.

breakthrough: An important discovery or advance in knowledge.

cholera: A disease caused by bacteria that causes severe diarrhea and vomiting.

disease: A sickness, especially one with specific symptoms or which affects a specific part of the body.

germs: Microscopic living things, especially those which cause disease.

germ theory: The belief that infectious disease results from the action of living things.

hand sanitizer: A liquid or gel applied to the hands to reduce the spread of disease-causing organisms.

identified: Found out what something was.

microorganisms: Life forms, such as viruses, bacteria, or fungi, that are so small they must be seen with a microscope.

polluted: Contaminated, especially with man-made waste.

PPE: Personal protective equipment, such as gloves, masks, and face shields.

theories: Beliefs or principles proposed to explain events of the natural world.

tuberculosis: A disease caused by bacteria that occurs mostly in a person's lungs.

INDEX

TO LEARN MORE

Finding more information is as easy as 1, 2, 3.

1 Go to www.factsurfer.com

2 Enter "germtheory" into the search box.

3 Choose your book to see a list of websites.

FACT SURFER